HARM'S WAY

Mac Wellman

BROADWAY PLAY PUBLISHING INC
New York
www.broadwayplaypublishing.com
info@broadwayplaypublishing.com

HARM'S WAY

First printing, this edition: March 2008

I S B N: 978-0-88145-379-9

Book design: Marie Donovan
Word processing: Word
Typographic controls: Ventura Publisher
Typeface: Palatino
Printed and bound in the U S A

HARM'S WAY is for Yolanda, with love

HARM'S WAY premiered on 13 November 1985 at the LaMama E T C Annex in New York, with the following cast:

MOTHER .... Tom Costello
FISHEYE .... Sheila Dabney
SANTOUCHE .... Stephen Mellor
ISLE OF MERCY .... Deirdre O'Connell
BY WAY OF BEING HIDDEN .... Zivia Flomenhaft
CROWSFOOT .... Gregg Daniel
WIZARD .... Shelia Dabney
BLACKMANGE .... Tom Costello
PRESIDENT MCKINLEY .... Jeff Shoemaker
CHORUSTuwanda Coleman, Amy Sobin, Lute Ramblin'

Director .... George Ferencz
Set design .... Patrick Kennedy
Costumes .... Sally Lesser
Lights .... Howard Thies
Stage manager .... Virlana Tkacz

Bob Jewett and Jack Maeby composed the music, which they performed along with Jeremy Kahn.

CHARACTERS

(in order of appearance)

MOTHER, *a firm believer in parental discipline*
CHILD, *a petulant brat*
FISHEYE, *a friend to*
SANTOUCHE, *an angry person*
ISLE OF MERCY, *his lady*
BY WAY OF BEING HIDDEN, *a person of curious identity*
CROWSFOOT, *an entrepreneur*
CROWSFOOT'S HELPER, *ditto*
POPSTAR, *an enterprising musician*
A MAN, *with a puzzling sense of humor*
WIZARD, *a specialist in an unlikely profession*
BLACKMANGE, *a man with important information*

and a CHORUS *of musicians in many guises*

Scene One

(An alley between darkened tenements. The MOTHER *is chasing her* CHILD *about in an attempt to get him to eat a sandwich she is holding in one hand. She has a revolver in her pocket.)*

MOTHER: Ugly kid. Eat!

CHILD: Witch. Go stuff it.

MOTHER: Watch your mouth.

CHILD: Don't want that crap. It's crap.

MOTHER: Good American cheese. Real baloney on Wonderbread. Eat it. Or else.

CHILD: Crap.

MOTHER: You don't eat it and I'll whip you good.

CHILD: Crap sandwich.

MOTHER: I'll show your ass.

CHILD: Stuff it up your ass, witch.

MOTHER: You don't eat that sandwich and I'll kill you good.

CHILD: Suck my dingus, witch.

MOTHER: Lemme at you, I'll bust your chops.

CHILD: Nyah! Nyah!

MOTHER: Kid don't talk to his mother like that. I'll teach you, little son of a bitch.

(She shoots and kills him.)

MOTHER: No respect...

(FISHEYE enters.)

FISHEYE: What's going on?

MOTHER: Little shit-ass wouldn't eat his sandwich, and I showed him.

(SANTOUCHE enters.)

SANTOUCHE: Hey, you.

MOTHER: No goddam respect...

SANTOUCHE: What's happening here? Who's the stiff?

MOTHER: Kid, that's all. None of your business.

SANTOUCHE: What happened, Fisheye?

FISHEYE: She and the kid were
fighting and then she
pulls the gun out and
shoots him, Santouche.
I never seen anything
like it.

SANTOUCHE: Fucking monster...

MOTHER: Guess I showed him.

FISHEYE: Santouche, what's wrong?

SANTOUCHE: Shut up.

MOTHER: No fucking respect.

SANTOUCHE: You really do that?

MOTHER: No fucking respect.

SANTOUCHE: Lady, I was talking to you.

MOTHER: HE DIDN'T HAVE NO FUCKING RESPECT.

SANTOUCHE: I asked you a question, bitch.

FISHEYE: Santouche...

SANTOUCHE: Shut up.

MOTHER: Leave me alone, big shot.
You got no respect either.

SANTOUCHE: I'll show you respect, bitch.

(He shoots and kills her.)

FISHEYE: Santouche!

SANTOUCHE: Fucking unnatural cunt. I can't stand 'em.

FISHEYE: Santouche, are you crazy?

SANTOUCHE: Killed her own flesh and blood.
Won't eat his sandwich, my ass!

FISHEYE: Santouche, let's get the hell out of here.

SANTOUCHE: All in good time.

CHORUS: *(Crying out)* What's going on? What's all the noise? Someone's been shot.

SANTOUCHE: Let's haul ass
out of here.

FISHEYE: Santouche...

SANTOUCHE: Move it, Fisheye, move it!

Scene Two

(The interior of a small, sparsely furnished house. ISLE OF MERCY *is seated at a table.* SANTOUCHE *is pacing back and forth.)*

ISLE OF MERCY: What's wrong?

SANTOUCHE: I've got to go away for a while.

ISLE OF MERCY: Why?

SANTOUCHE: I killed somebody. Had to. Didn't particularly want to, but I did. So

I've got to go someplace where I'll
be safe. Quiet.

ISLE OF MERCY: How long?

SANTOUCHE: Don't know.

ISLE OF MERCY: What am I supposed to do?

SANTOUCHE: Not your problem, Isle of Mercy.

ISLE OF MERCY: Don't call me that.

SANTOUCHE: It's funny. Isle of Mercy.
A pretty name for a pretty woman.

(He moves to embrace her.)

ISLE OF MERCY: It's not my name.

SANTOUCHE: It's your name if I say it is.
You got a better one?

ISLE OF MERCY: You know it.

SANTOUCHE: I need money. I'll have to sell
my things. Need money quick.

ISLE OF MERCY: How long?

SANTOUCHE: Lay off? I'm hassled enough.

ISLE OF MERCY: I am simply trying to figure out
what to do. That's all. How can
I know what to do otherwise?

SANTOUCHE: Talk too much. I need money.

ISLE OF MERCY: We don't have it.

SANTOUCHE: Have to sell something.
You have to sell something
for me.

ISLE OF MERCY: What? But what?

SANTOUCHE: The watch.

ISLE OF MERCY: It's broken.

SANTOUCHE: It's a gold watch.

ISLE OF MERCY: It stopped working a long time ago.

SANTOUCHE: You never wound it. It runs. It's a
gold watch. A thing like that's got
to be worth something. Where is it?

ISLE OF MERCY: Here. In the box.

SANTOUCHE: Let me see it, stupid.

ISLE OF MERCY: Watch what you say.

SANTOUCHE: Let me see the damn watch.

ISLE OF MERCY: It's broken.

SANTOUCHE: You never wound it right.

ISLE OF MERCY: How do you wind a watch wrong?

SANTOUCHE: You wound it backwards. I saw you.

ISLE OF MERCY: I never touched it.

SANTOUCHE: You did too.

ISLE OF MERCY: I never touched it. It's yours.

SANTOUCHE: I'll wind it up.

ISLE OF MERCY: Go ahead.

SANTOUCHE: Shut up.

ISLE OF MERCY: Leave me alone.

SANTOUCHE: It won't wind.

ISLE OF MERCY: I told you.

SANTOUCHE: You told me nothing. It's broken.

ISLE OF MERCY: I told you.

SANTOUCHE: I need money. What am I going to do...

ISLE OF MERCY: Sell it anyhow. It's gold, like you say.

SANTOUCHE: Not worth crap.

ISLE OF MERCY: Sure it is, even broken.

SANTOUCHE: Shut up.

ISLE OF MERCY: It's worth something. I'll sell it for you.

SANTOUCHE: I've got to get out of here.

ISLE OF MERCY: It'll be all right.

SANTOUCHE: Easy for you to say.

ISLE OF MERCY: I'm trying to help.

SANTOUCHE: Big help you are.

ISLE OF MERCY: I'll sell the watch and get the money to you.

SANTOUCHE: They'll throw me in the can.
I won't go again. Had enough.
It's too much. They'll have to
kill me first.

ISLE OF MERCY: Shut up.

SANTOUCHE: I won't go.

ISLE OF MERCY: Won't have to go if I sell the watch.

SANTOUCHE: I'll try it.

ISLE OF MERCY: Cheer up.

SANTOUCHE: How long will it take?

ISLE OF MERCY: A couple of days at most.

SANTOUCHE: Meet me at the Fair. Take the boat cross the river.

ISLE OF MERCY: How long?

SANTOUCHE: Two days. At sundown. By the Fair.

ISLE OF MERCY: All right.

SANTOUCHE: Bring the money. I'll be hiding.

ISLE OF MERCY: How'll I find you?

SANTOUCHE: I'll find you. I'll look different.

ISLE OF MERCY: I'll be there with the money.

SANTOUCHE: I'm all packed.

ISLE OF MERCY: Santouche.

SANTOUCHE: That's all. Have to get the hell
out of here. Bring the money. Once
the heat's off I'll be back. Maybe
I'll be lucky.

ISLE OF MERCY: Santouche...

SANTOUCHE: Have to go now. Don't bother me...

ISLE OF MERCY: Who'd you kill?

SANTOUCHE: Don't give me any trouble. I can't
take it. Just bring me the money. And
don't you mess around while I'm gone
or there'll be trouble, real trouble.

ISLE OF MERCY: Santouche!

SANTOUCHE: Told you I have to go.

(He leaves. She examines the watch more closely.)

ISLE OF MERCY: No wonder it's broken. There's some
kind of big, long hair in here. All
tangled and twisted up. Funny-looking thing.
(She pulls out the mainspring.)
Now look what I've done. It's more
broken now than it was before.

Scene Three

(A nightmarish hillside. Dim fires and explosions in the distance. There are three tall poles, or posts, on top of which are mounted wagon wheels. BY WAY OF BEING HIDDEN *and two dummies are strapped, respectively, atop each of these.)*

SANTOUCHE: What are you doing up there? Hey, you! They must be some apples in that tree...

BY WAY OF BEING HIDDEN: Sombitch, let me down outta here, hey stupid!

SANTOUCHE: Who're you calling stupid?

BY WAY OF: You, asshole. Let me down.

SANTOUCHE: And what if I don't want to?

BY WAY OF: For Christsake, man!

SANTOUCHE: How come you got up there
in the first place?

BY WAY OF: It's all part of the show.

SANTOUCHE: What show?

BY WAY OF: Never mind. Just let me down.

SANTOUCHE: Why should I bust my ass?

BY WAY OF: Look, I'll do good by you, you'll see.
You let me down and I'll even it up,
don't you worry about that. A man like me
you can trust, I swear.

SANTOUCHE: Well, how do I get you down?

BY WAY OF: I'll show you...

SANTOUCHE: What about them?

BY WAY OF: Croaked, you numbskull.

SANTOUCHE: I don't know about this...

BY WAY OF: Chickenshit, dumb chickenshit!

SANTOUCHE: What, who are you calling chickenshit, you?!

BY WAY OF: You, chickenshit, you're afraid
to climb this pole.

SANTOUCHE: Hell if I am.

BY WAY OF: You are.

SANTOUCHE: What's your name, anyhow?

BY WAY OF: By Way of Being Hidden.

SANTOUCHE: No, I asked for your name.

BY WAY OF: By Way of Being Hidden. That's my
name. Now get a move on, chickenshit, or come dark and the rats'll
gnaw my eyes out.

SANTOUCHE: Shit if I care. What kind of name is that?

BY WAY OF: Son, what is your name?

SANTOUCHE: Santouche.

BY WAY OF: Santouche, my friend, much as I
enjoy the pleasures of conversation,
and like yourself, no doubt, would never
presume upon the honorable disinterest
of a true friend.

SANTOUCHE: Get to the point.

BY WAY OF: Are you going to let me down, chickenshit?

SANTOUCHE: All in good time. You got money?

BY WAY OF: You think if I had money I'd've
got myself strapped up here, like a
goddamn human scarecrow?

SANTOUCHE: You said it was part of the show.

BY WAY OF: Santouche, I swear I will richly repay your generosity if you only shinny up this pole and cut these straps, you'll see, I'm not bullshitting.

SANTOUCHE: Well, all right, just let me figure out a safe way of getting up there.

BY WAY OF: For Jesus Christ's sake, there isn't any safe way of getting up here. Don't think, Santouche. Just do it. Don't you have no spirit of adventure?

SANTOUCHE: By Way of Being Hidden, my ass.

(Pause)

BY WAY OF: I'm a girl.

(Pause)

SANTOUCHE: Be right up.

Scene Four

(A small group of circus wagons and a tent in a clearing in the forest. The CHORUS *comes on stage and acts as an audience for* CROWSFOOT*'s exhortations.)*

CROWSFOOT: Ladies and gents! This is the final call!

ISLE OF MERCY: What's going on here?

CHORUS: We're waiting for the Guyanousa. They've got one in that tent...

CROWSFOOT: Ladies and gents! This is the final call for to get a glimpse at one of the most astonishing marvels ever presented 'neath the blue of God's welkin; a creature so rare it has never come across another like it, a creature so fabulous it has never even heard tell of itself, a creature

so lopsided—with the feet longer on one
side than the t'other—that it can graze
on the steepest mountain slope; and—
Ladies and gents, there is so much more
to be gleaned about this creature: some of it
scandalous, some of it horrifying, and all
of it amazing, at the very least! And
two bits, a measly one-quarter of a dollar,
will buy you admission to the tent, where
even now the creature is snorting and
stamping and shaking his shaggy locks. So,
if there's anyone out there who'd still
like a ticket he'd better holler because,
ladies and gents, this is the last call. And
them that miss this shot to see the fabulous
one-time-only legendary Guyanousa may have to
wait twenty, thirty, who knows how many years before
another such opportunity presents itself. So it's last
call, ladies and gents. Last call! Last call!
Last call!

ISLE OF MERCY: Sir, I'd like a ticket. Me, I'd like a ticket.

CROWSFOOT'S HELPER: Mister Crowsfoot...

CROWSFOOT: Yes, my dear, you come right over here, and I'll give you your ticket.

CROWSFOOT'S HELPER: Mister Crowsfoot!

CROWSFOOT: Yes, Mr. Suggs?

CROWSFOOT'S HELPER: Hot damn, Mister Crowsfoot! The Guyanousa am loose!

CROWSFOOT: Holy Jesus Mother of Mary I'm getting out of here!

CROWSFOOT'S HELPER: AYEEEEE!

CROWSFOOT: Last time it got loose it ate up
the whole town of Dead Snake Junction,
dogcatcher and all!

CROWSFOOT'S HELPER: The Guyanousa am loose!

(Crowd flees, screaming.)

CROWSFOOT'S HELPER: The Guyanousa am loose!

(HELPER *runs into the tent.* ISLE OF MERCY *stays.)*

CROWSFOOT: The Guyanousa am loose! *(Pause)*
Little lady, hadn't you better
run off, too? You don't want to get
eaten up, or—God forbid!—molested... *(Pause)*
by an ugly, evil-smelling,
hellfire-breathing, tree-uprooting
creature with no respect, that
ain't never been housebroken,
tamed, or other wise civilized,
now do you?

ISLE OF MERCY: I paid my quarter. I want to see
The Guyanousa.

CROWSFOOT: We can't hold it off forever,
can we, Mister Suggs? Mister Suggs?
The Lord be praised, it must've
already ate up Mister Suggs!
You'd better haul ass out of here,
young lady. Creature's got a strange
hankering for the innards of young
girls. Terrible things happened
in the last town, I assure you...

ISLE OF MERCY: I paid. I want to see.

CROWSFOOT: Young lady wants to see the Guyanosa,
Mr. Suggs, ain't that rich!
The Guyanousa am loose!
Don't you understand, young lady?

You'll be killed, tore up, massacreed.
God, what a bloody mess there'll be:
gore and blood and ruination a-
hanging from the treetops.

ISLE OF MERCY: I won't go till I see the Guyanousa.

CROWSFOOT: She won't go, Mister Suggs, do you
hear me? Till she catches sight
of the Guyanousa. Maybe we'd
just better oblige her. Do you
hear me, Mr. Suggs? She wants
to see the flaming Guyanousa! Suggs!
Pardon me, young lady, I'll just
tiptoe in the tent and see what awful
fate has befallen my colleague.

ISLE OF MERCY: There ain't no Guyanousa. You're a liar.

CROWSFOOT: Oh, now, don't say that.

ISLE OF MERCY: That was my last quarter.
I want to see the Guyanousa.

CROWSFOOT: You'll be ate up. Scram.

ISLE OF MERCY: You're a cheat.

CROWSFOOT: Beat it, bitch.

ISLE OF MERCY: Give me my money back.

CROWSFOOT: Get lost.

ISLE OF MERCY: I need the quarter. Otherwise
I can't cross the river.

CROWSFOOT: What river?

ISLE OF MERCY: Chagrin River.

CROWSFOOT: There's no river. Someone's diddled you.

ISLE OF MERCY: Sure there is. Chagrin River.

CROWSFOOT: It's part of the show. The con.

ISLE OF MERCY: Give me my quarter back.

CROWSFOOT: Go whistle for it.

ISLE OF MERCY: I don't have any money left.

CROWSFOOT: No skin off my teeth.

ISLE OF MERCY: You're a liar.

CROWSFOOT: Sucker born every day.

ISLE OF MERCY: I'm no sucker. Give me my money back.

CROWSFOOT: Get out of here.

ISLE OF MERCY: You're a crook.

CROWSFOOT: Honest as any man
can afford to be. A man's
got to live.

ISLE OF MERCY: Heard that before.

CROWSFOOT: Cynic. Beat it.

ISLE OF MERCY: Not till I get my money back.
I've got to have that quarter.

CROWSFOOT: I told you: there ain't no
such thing as any Anger River.
It's part of the show.

ISLE OF MERCY: Got to sell my watch and meet
my man on the other side.

CROWSFOOT: He must be part of the con, too.

ISLE OF MERCY: If he was here you wouldn't
say that.

CROWSFOOT: You don't beat it and I'll turn
the dogs loose on you.

ISLE OF MERCY: Why not the Guyanousa?

CROWSFOOT: What?

ISLE OF MERCY: You're a filthy liar.

CROWSFOOT: It's an honest day's work. That's all.

ISLE OF MERCY: I want my quarter back.

CROWSFOOT: There's other ways to get it.

ISLE OF MERCY: What do you mean?

CROWSFOOT: You're young yet. You can earn it
on your back.

ISLE OF MERCY: You cheated me.

CROWSFOOT: Nothing special about you.
Are you clean? Still, who'd
want to put it in you?

ISLE OF MERCY: I don't do things like that.

CROWSFOOT: Still, you're not much to look at.
You could be a gypsy and read
hands. Can you read hands?

ISLE OF MERCY: Give me my quarter.

CROWSFOOT: Look, bitch. I am trying to help you.

ISLE OF MERCY: Won't do it.

CROWSFOOT: If you had a beard.

ISLE OF MERCY: Just give me my quarter.

CROWSFOOT: Can you walk on your hands?

ISLE OF MERCY: Bastard.

CROWSFOOT: Here's my card. I am The Guyanousa.
Look, my dear, you'd better make up
your mind and make it up quick. If
you're not part of the show, you're
part of them that takes it all in,
and that's a fool. Think it over.

ISLE OF MERCY: What am I going to do?

CROWSFOOT: You're wasting my time.

ISLE OF MERCY: Bastard.

CROWSFOOT: Think it over.

(She sits down on the ground.)

Scene Five

(The POPSTAR *resembles a scarecrow tied to a stake. He holds an enormous guitar. As he sings he moves only his head and hands. Long pauses between stanzas. Again, the members of the* CHORUS *act as an audience. All are mounted on short stilts, and they lean together to form a human tripod. When the* POPSTAR *sings they moan and sway gently back and forth.* SANTOUCHE *and* BY WAY OF BEING HIDDEN *sit on the ground listening to the music.)*

POPSTAR:
You got to
You got to
You got to
You got to
You got to

You got to
You got to
You got to
You got to
You got to
Fry your head,
You got to
Fuck the dead.

You got to
You got to
You got to
You got to
You got to

You got to
You got to
You got to
Be what you
Think you want
To be if you
Want to know
Who plays what
Part in the show.

You got to
Get out
My way.
You got to
Move away,
You got to
Do what I
Say when I
Say what
My way is,
You got to
Do what I say
'Cause my way's
Harm's way.
(Repeat more softly, till end of scene)

BY WAY OF: You like it?

SANTOUCHE: What say?

BY WAY OF: You deaf?

SANTOUCHE: What say?

BY WAY OF: You deaf?

SANTOUCHE: What say?

BY WAY OF: Dead head.

SANTOUCHE: After what I done for you, how come you're not more grateful?

BY WAY OF: Brought you to the show,
didn't I? That's grateful.

SANTOUCHE: I am a man...

BY WAY OF: You ain't so special.

SANTOUCHE: Find yourself another. *(He gets up.)*

BY WAY OF: Hey, I didn't mean it.

SANTOUCHE: Fuck yourself. If this
is the show, it sucks.

BY WAY OF: Brought you to the show.
What did you expect?

SANTOUCHE: Music.

BY WAY OF: This is music.

SANTOUCHE: I mean music
music. This sucks.

BY WAY OF: What the hell do you expect from me?

SANTOUCHE: Nothing. I'm going. So long.
(He gets up.)

BY WAY OF: Hey, Santouche. Hey, man.
You gonna walk out on me?

SANTOUCHE: There's a place I've got to be at
by tomorrow. Other side of the river.

BY WAY OF: Other side of the river? You're crazy.

SANTOUCHE: I'm going.

BY WAY OF: What for? What for?
(He goes out.)
Shaddup!

(Music stops. Pause)

BY WAY OF: Nobody runs out on me.
(Pause)

Wonder what's so hot
on the other side of the river.

Scene Six

(In front of an old saloon. Noise of conversation and merriment from within. As he attempts to enter, SANTOUCHE *bumps into* FISHEYE, *who is leaving. Later on in the scene, the* COOK *is played by a member of the* CHORUS.*)*

SANTOUCHE: Fisheye! What're you doing
this side of the river?
I thought you'd be long gone by now.

FISHEYE: Lucky I found you. You can't
go in there. Blackmange is having
a party. It's his birthday.

SANTOUCHE: Thought I smelled something
that stunk.

FISHEYE: You gotta be real careful.

SANTOUCHE: How many men's he got with him?

FISHEYE: Only nine.

SANTOUCHE: Armed?

FISHEYE: Knives, sidearms, grenades.

SANTOUCHE: Can you cover me
from the kitchen?

FISHEYE: You can't be serious.

SANTOUCHE: Fisheye, I'm going in there.

FISHEYE: They'll massacree ya.

SANTOUCHE: Not if you help.

FISHEYE: What's your plan?

SANTOUCHE: Go around back to the kitchen.

FISHEYE: Won't be a party to this.
(SANTOUCHE pulls a gun on him.)
Anything you say, Santouche.

SANTOUCHE: Remember all the good
I done ya.

FISHEYE: You're right. I ought to be more
grateful. We'll get 'em in the
crossfire.

SANTOUCHE: Blackmange! I don't believe it!

FISHEYE: It's him all right.

SANTOUCHE: After all these years!

FISHEYE: What happens if they decide
to bust out the back way?

SANTOUCHE: I'll cut 'em down before
they get to you.

FISHEYE: All right then.

SANTOUCHE: I'll start after you fire the
first shot, only lay off old
Blackmange himself. I want him.

(FISHEYE rushes out as BY WAY OF BEING HIDDEN enters from saloon, slightly drunk.)

BY WAY OF: Santouche, is that you?

SANTOUCHE: You clear out of here if you
want to stay alive.

BY WAY OF: It's a matter of some importance.

SANTOUCHE: Back off, bitch, or you're a dead
man.

BY WAY OF: You saved my life. I mean
I was only trying to help. But
seeing as how... *(She backs off.)*

SANTOUCHE: That's better. Now you just stay there
till me and my friend are finished.

BY WAY OF: Fine with me.

SANTOUCHE: Blackmange, you asshole!

*(*FISHEYE *begins to fire. Yells and screams from within.* SANTOUCHE *begins to fire through windows and doors of the saloon.)*

SANTOUCHE: Blackmange!

*(*BLACKMANGE *stumbles through the door. Slumps.* SANTOUCHE *shoots him several times.* BLACKMANGE *falls and lies motionless. Shooting subsides.)*

SANTOUCHE: Got him, Fisheye! I got him. Hey,
Fisheye, I got him. He's dead. Just
look at him. Stinking, ugly stiff.
Whoopee! Hey, Fisheye...

*(*COOK *enters.)*

COOK: He's dead.

SANTOUCHE: Dead? Fisheye?

COOK: The whole gang went busting out the
back way. You kept pluggin' the stiff.
They ripped him up good. He's dead. They're
gone. They'll come back for you, Santouche.

SANTOUCHE: Get lost.

COOK: They'll do a number on you. *(Goes out)*

BY WAY OF: Santouche, hey.

SANTOUCHE: What is it?

BY WAY OF: Remember me?

SANTOUCHE: Beat it.

BY WAY OF: You saved my life.

SANTOUCHE: My friend's croaked, can't you see? Beat it.

BY WAY OF: Your lady's been abducted.

SANTOUCHE: What!

BY WAY OF: That's right.

SANTOUCHE: Who? Where?

BY WAY OF: Don't know.

SANTOUCHE: Shit if you don't know. Some kind of trick this is. You don't tell me who's got her and...

BY WAY OF: Easy now.
I don't know who's got her,
but I do know who does know...

SANTOUCHE: Who's that?

BY WAY OF: Him.

SANTOUCHE: The stiff.

BY WAY OF: Yep.

SANTOUCHE: Blackmange?

BY WAY OF: Yup. You killed him.

SANTOUCHE: Why didn't you tell me?

BY WAY OF: I tried.

SANTOUCHE: You didn't try hard enough.

BY WAY OF: What am I supposed to do?

SANTOUCHE: Shut up.

BY WAY OF: But fortunately I have an idea.

SANTOUCHE: Shut up. How do I know
you're telling me the truth
about Isle of Mercy?

BY WAY OF: Don't believe me then. I don't give a crap.

SANTOUCHE: She was going to sell my watch.

BY WAY OF: Going around with all that money on her.

SANTOUCHE: So what?

BY WAY OF: All alone from what I hear.

SANTOUCHE: So?

BY WAY OF: You want to hear my idea?

SANTOUCHE: No. Beat it.

BY WAY OF: All right.
Just trying to be of use.
Didn't mean no harm.

SANTOUCHE: Get lost. Leave me alone. Beat it.

BY WAY OF: Be seeing you.

SANTOUCHE: What the hell am I going to do?

BY WAY OF: Want to hear my idea?

SANTOUCHE: Beat it, lady, or I'll lay you out
for the buzzards.

BY WAY OF: Okay. Okay. Just trying to help...
(She starts to go out and pauses.)
I got a friend who's got a friend as
can make that stiff talk. It's true.

SANTOUCHE: What'd you say?

Scene Seven

(A starry night. ISLE OF MERCY *sits on a boulder looking at the moon. She sings her song.)*

ISLE OF MERCY: This is
Isle of Mercy's song.
It won't be long.

She is very
very tough.
She got no inside,
got no outside.
Whoever told you so,
they lied.

(The two CHILDREN *are at first hidden in the shadows. They approach her gingerly, and only after a rather long pause.)*

FIRST CHILD: Hey, lady.

(Pause)

SECOND CHILD: Hey, lady,
what are you doing?

ISLE OF MERCY: Looking at stars.

(Pause)

SECOND CHILD: I said what are you doing?

ISLE OF MERCY: I said looking
at stars. Can't you hear? *(Pause)*
That light
up there.
That's a star.

SECOND CHILD: Ain't you lonely
sitting there?

ISLE OF MERCY: Nope... Sometimes.

(Pause)

FIRST CHILD: I got a rock with a face on it.

(Pause)

FIRST CHILD: I got a rock with a face on it.

ISLE OF MERCY: I heard you the first time.

(Pause)

FIRST CHILD: You want to see it? *(Pause)*
You want to see it?

(Pause)

ISLE OF MERCY: Okay. Show me the rock
with the face on it.
(She examines the rock.)
That ain't no face...

SECOND CHILD: I told you that wasn't no face.

FIRST CHILD: Sure looks like it to me. *(Pause)*
The moon's got a face, see.

(They all look up briefly.)

FIRST CHILD: Sometimes he turns his face
to one side. Sometimes it's
straight on. I can't see
too good. It's awful far.

SECOND CHILD: He can't see straight.

ISLE OF MERCY: I was talking to him.
You don't need to butt in.

FIRST CHILD: The moon's a rock with
a face on it.

ISLE OF MERCY: Pretty big rock, if it's just a rock. *(Pause)*
Whose kids are you
anyhow? Crowsfoot's?

SECOND CHILD: Hell no...

FIRST CHILD: We borned ourselves
out of rocks.

ISLE OF MERCY: Kids don't come
from rocks, stupid.

FIRST CHILD: Shit, I know that.

ISLE OF MERCY: Where do they come from?

FIRST CHILD: You know...

(CROWSFOOT *enters.)*

CROWSFOOT: Well my dear, are my little
self-begotten bastards bothering
you? If they grieve you, take a
stone to 'em.

ISLE OF MERCY: Go back to the wagon, Crowsfoot.

CROWSFOOT: They's a customer. You come along.

ISLE OF MERCY: I am relaxing
with my friends.

CROWSFOOT: The Wheel of Possibility don't slow down
for nobody nohow, that's for sure.
You rattle your bones, and get a move on.
Hup, hup!

ISLE OF MERCY: Scram, Crowsfoot.

CROWSFOOT: Pretty lady, you are pushing me
to extreme acts of unkind coercion.

*(*ISLE OF MERCY *stands up on tiptoe and peers offstage as though to catch a glimpse of the prospective customer. Then she sits back down. Pause)*

ISLE OF MERCY: I won't do it.

CROWSFOOT: Yes you will.

ISLE OF MERCY: No I won't.

CROWSFOOT: Yes you will

ISLE OF MERCY: Think you can tell me what to do!

CROWSFOOT: You'll do exactly what I tell you to.

(Pause)

ISLE OF MERCY: Shit on you.

CROWSFOOT: Watch your mouth.

ISLE OF MERCY: I won't do it.

CROWSFOOT: Yes you will.

ISLE OF MERCY: You fuck him then.

CROWSFOOT: Now Mercy, cool down...

ISLE OF MERCY: You know who that is?

CROWSFOOT: He's just like everybody else.

ISLE OF MERCY: That is the devil himself.

CROWSFOOT: So? I'm not particular.

ISLE OF MERCY: I am.

CROWSFOOT: You can't afford it.

ISLE OF MERCY: Oh yes I can. Like
the man said, There is
some shit I do not
eat.

(Pause)

CROWSFOOT: You want me to give
you another one of my
speechifications?

(Pause)

ISLE OF MERCY: You win.

CROWSFOOT: Come along then.

*(*CROWSFOOT *leaves.* ISLE OF MERCY *gets up to go.)*

ISLE OF MERCY: So long.

BOTH CHILDREN: So long.

(Pause. ISLE OF MERCY *sits back down.)*

FIRST CHILD: Moon's where the ghosts go.

ISLE OF MERCY: Why do they do that?

FIRST CHILD: So no one can hurt them.

SECOND CHILD: Who can hurt a ghost,
stupid? A ghost's a dead
thing. It don't have to
be protected.

(Pause)

ISLE OF MERCY: Maybe the moon's a ghost...

SECOND CHILD: You ever seen a ghost?

FIRST CHILD: What do you mean by that?

SECOND CHILD: I'm getting scared.
Come on, let's go
back to the wagon.

CROWSFOOT: *(Offstage)* Isle of Mercy!

ISLE OF MERCY: They ain't no such thing
as a ghost.

FIRST CHILD: Why'd you say that
about the moon being
a ghost.

SECOND CHILD: Let's go back, come on!

ISLE OF MERCY: I don't know.

FIRST CHILD: You talk funny. For a girl.

ISLE OF MERCY: You know what I'd do
if I was a ghost?

CROWSFOOT: *(Offstage.)* Isle of Mercy!

SECOND CHILD: I'm getting out of here!

FIRST CHILD: If I was a ghost I'd
fly away. Fly right smack
out of here. That's for damn sure.

SECOND CHILD: You're both crazy. *(Goes out. Pause)*

Scene Eight

(A clearing in the forest. BY WAY OF BEING HIDDEN, SANTOUCHE, *a* WIZARD, *and the corpse of* BLACKMANGE. *The* WIZARD *is dressed as the others except he sports a necklace of onions, garlic, and rattlesnake skins. His top hat is festooned with leafy twigs and switches. He carries a small black bag full of bottles and tins.* BY WAY OF BEING HIDDEN *carries a large suitcase. To revive* BLACKMANGE *the* WIZARD *kneads a paste from the flour, water, and whiskey. He then rolls the paste into a little ball, plants a garlic clove in the ball, and places it under the dead man's tongue.)*

WIZARD: That's the corpse.

BY WAY OF: Yup.

WIZARD: How'd he croak?

BY WAY OF: It wasn't measles.

WIZARD: How'd he croak?

BY WAY OF: Shot. Ah. Several times.

WIZARD: Uhm. So you say.

BY WAY OF: Can you do it?

WIZARD: Maybe.

SANTOUCHE: Well? Can he do it?

BY WAY OF: Says maybe.

SANTOUCHE: Shit.

WIZARD: I'll need some
flour, water, and
a bottle of whiskey.

BY WAY OF: Coming right up. *(Rummages through the suitcase for these)*

SANTOUCHE: What you gonna do?

WIZARD: Like patching a tire.

BY WAY OF: Hear that, Santouche?
Like patching a tire!

SANTOUCHE: I hear it.

WIZARD: Is that the killer?

BY WAY OF: That's the killer.

WIZARD: Was there bad blood between?

BY WAY OF: You might say.

WIZARD: By Way of Being Hidden,
I don't want none of your
horse crap. This is serious
business. And you get that
man outta sight, hear?

BY WAY OF: Santouche, you get
out of sight, you hear?

SANTOUCHE: Why? I stand where I please,
as I please.

BY WAY OF: If the stiff sees you it won't work.

SANTOUCHE: Hell.

WIZARD: It's true, son.

SANTOUCHE: All right, all right, Shit, man!
Can't get no peace from a man
even by killing him no more.

WIZARD: This world
is full of dark souls
and wondrous things.

SANTOUCHE: What kind of sawbones
can bring a man back to life anyhow?

WIZARD: Young man, you are disturbing
me. This is America. Therefore
anything can happen...
Aside from which, the object is
not to restore the poor stiff
from across the murky deeps of
Styx, which is ridiculous;
but a more pragmatic and wholly
American one: namely, to bring
him temporarily back from across
the shadowy waters of Lethe.

SANTOUCHE: Afraid I lost you.

BY WAY OF: A stiff's a stiff.

WIZARD: What I mean is that all we need
is his memory. He don't have to
be alive, you dig?

SANTOUCHE: Yeah...but.

WIZARD: All we got to do is trick him
into thinking he's alive.

SANTOUCHE: Is that all...

WIZARD: That is the practical approach
to the art of undoing death.

SANTOUCHE: I'm afraid I still don't understand,
Doc, but I'll take your word for it.
All I want is results.

WIZARD: My sentiments exactly.

SANTOUCHE: By Way, I have a feeling he's bullshit.

BY WAY OF: Shut up, Santouche.

SANTOUCHE: That stiff don't know beans.

WIZARD: Shut up, killer.

SANTOUCHE: Only ones end up getting killed have had it coming. Like him.

WIZARD: Oh yeah? What'd he do?

SANTOUCHE: Spit in my eye. Told me off in front of people. Went and stooled on me good.

WIZARD: Concerning what?

SANTOUCHE: Never you mind. I spent some time out of circulation on account of him.

WIZARD: So you killed him.

SANTOUCHE: Let's just say he got his comeuppance.

WIZARD: Let's just say...

SANTOUCHE: You're a wise one, you are.

WIZARD: Gentlemen, we are about ready to begin The Con.

SANTOUCHE: What's he talking about?

BY WAY OF: What con is that, doc?

WIZARD: Friends, we are about to fool death himself. It's all part of the show.

BY WAY OF: Hot damn! He's serious.

SANTOUCHE: The man is out of his mind!

WIZARD: What's his name?

SANTOUCHE: Blackmange.

WIZARD: Blackmange? What kind of a name is that?

SANTOUCHE: It's because he's so ugly.

(The WIZARD *cradles* BLACKMANGE.*)*

WIZARD: Blackmange, my friend, are you awake?

SANTOUCHE: Nothing's happening.

BY WAY OF: Shut up.

WIZARD: Blackmange, sit up now, you've been
asleep for a long time, why it's past noon,
the birds are a-singing, sun is a-shining away,
pretty girls are a-wiggling their asses out in the street,
ain't you ever going to get up? Ain't you hungry?

BLACKMANGE: Ahhhhhh.

WIZARD: Blackmange, I'm going to do right by you,
I swear it, I'll kill 'em myself, whoever
it was done this to you, you'll see, who was it?
Tell me, Blackmange, and I'll nail 'em good, you'll see.

BLACKMANGE: Ahhhhhhhhh.

SANTOUCHE: Jesus fucking Christ.

BY WAY OF: Shut up.

WIZARD: Who done it, tell me, Blackmange?

BLACKMANGE: Dunno...

WIZARD: The girl, who's got the girl? Maybe
he done it, I'll get him for you, you'll
see, come on, Blackmange.

BLACKMANGE: Ahhhhhhhhhhhhhh.

WIZARD: Her name's Isle of Mercy.

BLACKMANGE: Santouche girl. He done it. He killed me.

WIZARD: What about the girl? Who's got her?

BLACKMANGE: He done it. Ahhhh.

WIZARD: I'll settle his apples, you bet I will,
but that girl, who's got her? That guy that's
got her's in on it, I swear, him and Santouche,
I swear, who was it?

BLACKMANGE: Santouche... and him?

WIZARD: Who was it? He's the real one, he set you up,
I swear he did, he was laughing at you, come on,
who was it, old Blackmange, only way for me to get
even, no, don't go back to sleep without telling me,
who's the man who's got Isle of Mercy?

BLACKMANGE: Guyanousa's got her.

WIZARD: What's that? What'd you say?

SANTOUCHE: Did you hear what he said?

BY WAY OF: I don't get it: guy snoozing....
What's that? I don't get it.

SANTOUCHE: Can you make out what it is?

WIZARD: Who's got her? Who was it, Blackmange?
He done you in, that one.

BLACKMANGE: Guyanousa's got her.

WIZARD: Guyanousa's got her. Now it clicks.
The Guyanousa is a sideshow con.

BY WAY OF: That's right. Now I remember.

SANTOUCHE: He said the Guyanousa's got her...

BLACKMANGE: Ahhhhhhh... kill him.

WIZARD: Fuck you stiff! Go back to being
dead. We're going to feed you to pigs.
Santouche's here, take a look at him.

SANTOUCHE: Fuck you, Blackmange.

BLACKMANGE: Ahhhh...

BY WAY OF: He's dead again.

WIZARD: He always was. Now he knows it again.

SANTOUCHE: The Guyanousa.

WIZARD: Friends, I'll be going now. Please
don't hesitate to get in touch if
you should ever require my services

again. I also raise storms, debase coin,
cause floods, stunt crops, induce a few
miscarriages, and on a good day I can
throw a close election.

SANTOUCHE: Here's your money, beat it.

WIZARD: Be seeing you, kind gentlefolk, be seeing you.
(Takes up his bag and goes out)

SANTOUCHE: No one does that to me.

BY WAY OF: What are you talking about?

SANTOUCHE: The Guyanousa.

BY WAY OF: Now aren't you glad
for the favor I done you?

SANTOUCHE: I'll get him good.

BY WAY OF: You don't sound grateful.

SANTOUCHE: Shit on you. Beat it.

BY WAY OF: Last time I ever help you out.

SANTOUCHE: Leave me alone, understand?

BY WAY OF: All right, all right, I didn't mean
anything by it. I'm going, I'm going...
(She starts to go out.)

SANTOUCHE: Fucking sideshow con-man.

BY WAY OF: Knew a man like you
once. One day a little
blue bug came up and
bit him on the ass.
He went nuts.
Beat himself to death
with his own fist.
(Pause. She slowly turns and exits.)

Scene Nine

(A hillside by the river. The river is filled with smoke. A small, mullioned window is planted on the hill, and dim light shines through. Old gravestones and stuffed rats are scattered about. The MAN *is standing in a waist-deep grave he has dug on the hill. His companion, a dummy, is propped against a nearby tree. The dummy's chest is pierced by several arrows, and there is a hatchet buried in his forehead.* SANTOUCHE *appears from behind the hill. He is crossing the river on stilts, and is dressed fantastically so that he resembles a giant bird. After greeting the* MAN, *he climbs down to the earth.)*

SANTOUCHE: All on a-fucking-count of the goddam watch that don't keep time, and that goddam woman that couldn't tell the fucking time if the goddam watch kept it. Wonder where the hell she is.

MAN: Hey, you! Shinbones!

SANTOUCHE: You talking to me, groundhog?

MAN: Yeah, you. Who'd you think I was talking to?

SANTOUCHE: What're you doing in that hole?

MAN: Well I'm not here
for my beauty sleep,
that's for sure. Come here.

SANTOUCHE: What's wrong with him?

MAN: Stiff. Can't you see? A fucking stiff.

SANTOUCHE: That much I can tell.

MAN: He was being difficult.

SANTOUCHE: What did you say?

MAN: It's why I killed him.

SANTOUCHE: I don't understand your meaning.

MAN: How would you, if I haven't
explained my meaning to you?

SANTOUCHE: Got a point there.

MAN: Thing is...

SANTOUCHE: Well, good day, sir. I think I'll
just mosey on down the road....
It's been a real pleasure.

(The MAN *pulls a gun on* SANTOUCHE.*)*

MAN: Hold on, buddy.

SANTOUCHE: You meet such interesting people...

MAN: One step further and I'll drill ya.

SANTOUCHE: Just a figure of speech.
I wasn't really planning to walk off
like that. After all, we haven't even
been properly introduced. My name's Santouche.

MAN: Now listen, bud, and listen good.... .
You listening?

SANTOUCHE: I'm listening. Real close...

MAN: This stiff is a stiff 'cause he won't
bury me. He wouldn't do it. So I
off him, and he still won't do it.
Seems simple enough to me. Shovel
a few yards of dirt over me. I told
him I'd lie real still, and not to
worry if I started to squirm around
once he got to my face. I told him
he could have my stuff. Shoes. Pack.
Good hat. And a couple guns. That's
not asking a whole lot, it seems
to me. Well, he had some kind of old-fashioned
ethical-humanist compunctions

about burying a living man. We talked it over for a long time. He threatened to take off without helping me out...

SANTOUCHE: I'll bury you, sure I will, no sweat.

MAN: Shut up. It's not polite to interrupt.

SANTOUCHE: Sorry. I was just trying to be neighborly.

MAN: I don't want you to bury me. I want him to.

SANTOUCHE: But he's dead...

MAN: That's where you come in.

SANTOUCHE: I'm afraid I don't get what you mean. Or maybe I'm just thick.

MAN: He won't listen to me.

SANTOUCHE: No, it doesn't look as though he'll do a whole lot of listening from here on in.

MAN: But you are listening to me.

SANTOUCHE: Oh yes, I certainly am, and it's a great pleasure to do so.

MAN: Then you talk to him.

SANTOUCHE: What?

MAN: I said you talk to him, and convince him he ought to do as I say.

SANTOUCHE: But, he's a stiff.

MAN: And you'd better be pretty goddam persuasive.

SANTOUCHE: You're pulling my leg.

MAN: Because if you don't talk that pigheaded son-of-a-bitch into burying me, I'm likely to get angry again, and I'll just have to blow you away for sure, and bud, you'll look as worse off as him. And that ain't good.

SANTOUCHE: No indeed, sir, it ain't good at all.

MAN: Well, what say, my young man?

SANTOUCHE: I guess I see it your way.

MAN: I'm so glad you listen to reason.

SANTOUCHE: Well, it's no trouble, my friend. I mean
I do like to be helpful, particularly to
one like yourself, who is so...

MAN: Persuasive...

SANTOUCHE: What's his name?

MAN: Cleveland. Mister Grover Cleveland.

SANTOUCHE: Thanks.

MAN: You're welcome, I'm sure.

SANTOUCHE: You're fortunate I've got some recent
experience in this field....
Ah, Mister Cleveland...

MAN: You don't need to be so formal.
A friend of mine's a friend of his.

SANTOUCHE: Oh, I see. Ah, Grover, old man.

MAN: That's better...

SANTOUCHE: Ah yes, Grover, my friend. I hear
you're unwilling to oblige our
common friend here, ah....
Might I ask what your name is, sir?

MAN: Surely. I'm called William McKinley.

SANTOUCHE: Ah, yes, Mister McKinley here desires
that I do my utmost to convince
you of the folly of your ways, in so
willfully resisting his blandishments
to the effect that you assist him in his

ardent wish to be—er—interred at this time, in this place...

MAN: That's very good.

SANTOUCHE: Thank you kindly, Mister McKinley, I'll just go on.

MAN: Don't let me interfere.

SANTOUCHE: Now, my dear Mister Cleveland, much as I do not wish to presume to offer unsolicited advice, especially in the case of so recent a friendship...

MAN: Very tactful. I like that....

(SANTOUCHE kicks the gun away and grabs it.)

MAN: Shit.

SANTOUCHE: Okay, stiff, get out of that hole, and get out of there quick.

MAN: It was only a joke.

SANTOUCHE: Joke my ass. Move!

MAN: Don't. Don't. Don't.

SANTOUCHE: Now grab that stiff, stiff, and throw him in the hole.

MAN: What're you so angry about? It was a joke. It's all in good spirits I assure you.

SANTOUCHE: Now you get in the hole.

MAN: What are you going to do?

SANTOUCHE: Just what you said you wanted.

MAN: You must be crazy.

SANTOUCHE: Shut up, Mister McKinley.

(Begins to shovel dirt over the MAN, who is by now back in the grave.)

MAN: It was a joke, just part of the show.
I was bored. Have pity on me. The future
is boredom. I wouldn't have harmed you, I
swear! It was all part of the show.

(SANTOUCHE *is shoveling rapidly now.)*

SANTOUCHE: Eat shit. Eat dirt. Eat shit. Dirt... shit... dirt...

MAN: But I'll suffocate. You can't be serious.

SANTOUCHE: Mr. McKinley, sir, my name is Santouche,
and I am very serious.

MAN: You're a monster.

SANTOUCHE: I'm doing you a favor. Get your head
down or I'll shoot your ears off. Get down...

MAN: Help, a monster!

(SANTOUCHE *kills him with the shovel.)*

SANTOUCHE: You're part of nobody's show now,
my friend.
(Finishes burying the MAN.*)*
Takes all kinds, my friend.
A man who fools with me hurts me,
and I'll be obliged to hate him. *(Pause)*
You started it, buster.
Won't go playing your tricks
on anyone else.... *(Pause)*
Guess I showed you. *(Pause)*
Wonder who the hell he was? *(Pause)*
Buried two presidents today!
First time I ever did that. *(Pause)*
...didn't mean no harm! My ass! *(Pause)*
...all part of the show. You are dead,
man, and I spit on your stiff, and
man, you can't do one blessed thing
about it! *(Pause)*

Wonder who the hell he was? *(Pause)*
...part of the show!

Scene Ten

(A circus wagon standing on an open plain. SANTOUCHE, *looking very exhausted, sits downstage. He takes off his boots and rubs his feet. The members of the* CHORUS *speak their lines in turn from their usual position just outside the main playing area.)*

FIRST CHORISTER: Guyanousa? I heard of it, but offhand I can't recall what it was I heard.

SECOND CHORISTER: Never heard of it. You must be crazy.

THIRD CHORISTER: I heard of it, but there ain't no such thing, of that I'm sure.

FIRST CHORISTER: Nope.

SECOND CHORISTER: Search me.

THIRD CHORISTER: Never heard of it.

FIRST CHORISTER: Guya-what?! You must be stewed!

SECOND CHORISTER: A story that's told by folks 'round here. Don't you pay it no nevermind.

THIRD CHORISTER: It's against the laws of nature for such a creature to exist. Of that I'm sure.

FIRST CHORISTER: Somebody pulling your leg, fella!

SECOND CHORISTER: But that was all part of the show. bud, they ain't nobody takes such things serious anymore.

THIRD CHORISTER: I hear there's wonderful strange creatures at the far end of the world. That's what I hear.

*(*CROWSFOOT *emerges from the wagon, walks downstage, and sits next to* SANTOUCHE.*)*

CROWSFOOT: My friend, mind if I sit down beside you?

SANTOUCHE: Nope.

CROWSFOOT: Crowsfoot's the name. What's yours?

SANTOUCHE: Santouche.

CROWSFOOT: You look beat.

SANTOUCHE: Yup.

CROWSFOOT: I bear good news.
(Pause)

SANTOUCHE: Go away.

CROWSFOOT: You're a fortunate man.

SANTOUCHE: Go away.

CROWSFOOT: I am the first ordained minister of the
Church of Christ Fornicator. No shit, it's true. And
I got my license right here. Now you, friend:
What woe has been your lot, who can tell? You
look like a disaster. What you need's a nice
little piece. Now you can get it, and get saved
at the same time. Ticket's only a quarter.
You don't want to miss out on a good thing, do you?

SANTOUCHE: Don't have no quarter.

CROWSFOOT: Come on, don't feel shy. It'd be
good for you. Buy your ticket. Climb
into my wagon there. My little madonna,
she's got fine moves, and my friend, it's
not every day you can get saved and laid
at the same time. Why, it's practically
miraculous. Only costs a quarter.

SANTOUCHE: Don't want no pussy.

CROWSFOOT: The Lord don't have much use for melancholia, my friend.

SANTOUCHE: Don't want it.

CROWSFOOT: How do you expect to get it if you don't want it?

SANTOUCHE: Fed up.

CROWSFOOT: You look like a fine, strapping man of god.
There is no point in all this down-and-out misery.
I'll tell you because I know from my own experience.
If you turn your heart to Christ Fornicator you will find untold bliss. Satisfaction guaranteed.
Once you get enlightenment anything is possible.
No one ever gonna shove your face in shit, no one ever gonna call you names! If you got it, friend, and I mean get it, you're gonna get laid both in body and soul!
With the Lord doing it in your heart, you're gonna have a big edge on the next man, friend, and in this evil son-of-a-bitch's world, full of conniving wildcats, you need every bit of edge you can get. Ain't it so, friend? Don't matter where it come from. How about it?

SANTOUCHE: Had enough. Don't want nothing.

CROWSFOOT: Now I was as empty and bitter as you are once, before I got religion. Then I put down my quarter, and all of a sudden, I saw that all my former life was spent in folly. And that squaring the circle of desire and completion was a cinch. *(Pause)*
What it comes down to, my friend, is quite simple:
YOU CAN HAVE WHAT YOU WANT! IT'S YOURS FOR THE ASKING!
Myself, I was part of he show, I am ashamed to say.
You look like you know whereof I am speaking.
I practiced deception on my fellow man. Now that all seems like a nightmare of some dark, grimy, brooding, sooty, barren, windswept country full of liars, cheats,

scoundrels, lunatics—monsters even—who all
look the same! The fools! And that nightmare was lit up
only by the fires of vengeance and hatred. Honestly,
one could gag.
Why, the terrible things I done! And youknow, I never
got laid!

SANTOUCHE: What was your con?

CROWSFOOT: I can see you're a child of darkness
still, my friend.

SANTOUCHE: Your con, what was it?

CROWSFOOT: Shameful, I cheated folk by pretending
to be a fabulous beast.

SANTOUCHE: I've done things like that. Are you for real?

CROWSFOOT: Do I not radiate gladness and
the joy of fulsome success?

SANTOUCHE: You smell like a bank of roses.

CROWSFOOT: My friend, why not let me enlist you right
this minute in our double-indemnified and wholly tax-deductible Church of Christ Fornicator, and lead
you to consummation devoutly to be wished?

(SANTOUCHE *gives a quarter to* CROWSFOOT.)

SANTOUCHE: What kind of beast were you?

CROWSFOOT: Let us not dwell on the antediluvian,
my friend, let me lead you instead up...

SANTOUCHE: Just curious, that's all. I was a killer.

CROWSFOOT: I see. Well. If I can't interest you, young
man, I guess I'll be seeing you. Aha! Yes...
(He gets up and looks at the watch, which is still sprung.)
It's getting late. Nevertheless, I wish you well.
Our paths may be different, but our hearts....

SANTOUCHE: Where did you get that watch?

CROWSFOOT: What! Why? This watch?

SANTOUCHE: The watch. Where did you get it?

CROWSFOOT: You do ask questions.

SANTOUCHE: Where.

CROWSFOOT: Ah...

SANTOUCHE: I think we have some matters to discuss, my friend.

CROWSFOOT: Oh, I wouldn't want to detain you any further.

SANTOUCHE: No trouble, I'm sure. Your little
presentation has stirred up quite a commotion
in my cynic breast.
and I am eager to learn more.

CROWSFOOT: I can tell by your bearing that you're a man of eminence. My poor insignificant surmises could be of no possible interest to one of your erudition and mental prowess. Therefore...

SANTOUCHE: On the contrary...
(Pulls out his gun.)

CROWSFOOT: You want your quarter back?

Scene Eleven

(The same as the previous scene. The circus wagon is turned upside down, and one wheel is spinning. It is nearly dark. The FIRST *and* SECOND CHILDREN, *who cry out at* SANTOUCHE, *are hidden behind boulders. They dart from one place to another as he tries to catch them.* SANTOUCHE *and* ISLE OF MERCY *stand facing each other as the scene begins.)*

SANTOUCHE: You, look at you, fucking whore.

ISLE OF MERCY: Got the money. Had to get the money.

SANTOUCHE: You, look at you.

ISLE OF MERCY: Couldn't sell the watch.
It was busted. Lost the quarter.

SANTOUCHE: Shut up.

ISLE OF MERCY: Here's the money.

SANTOUCHE: How come you stayed with him?

ISLE OF MERCY: You didn't have to kill him.

SANTOUCHE: After what he done?

ISLE OF MERCY: None of your business.

SANTOUCHE: You and him in on it together?

ISLE OF MERCY: Things don't always work out right.

SANTOUCHE: Shut up.

ISLE OF MERCY: You shut up. I got my pride.

SANTOUCHE: You got nothing. Except me.
And I don't know if I want you anymore.

(Pause)

ISLE OF MERCY: Here's the money. I'm leaving.

SANTOUCHE: What?

ISLE OF MERCY: Going.

SANTOUCHE: Sit down.

ISLE OF MERCY: I'm leaving. Going. I'm finished
with people mad all the time. Sick of it.
Like you.

SANTOUCHE: Who'd take you in?

ISLE OF MERCY: Don't bother me.
Who'd treat me worse? I used to love

you. Santouche, but you're a killer
and I'm sick of that.

SANTOUCHE: Bitch. Sit down. I told you.

ISLE OF MERCY: You eat shit, Santouche.

SANTOUCHE: Don't talk to me that way.

ISLE OF MERCY: Now I'm getting mad, Jesus!

SANTOUCHE: None of 'em got killed, but
had it coming, I assure you.

ISLE OF MERCY: World's a bad place, I know.

SANTOUCHE: So leave me be. Sit down.

ISLE OF MERCY: No, I don't want to. Too much,
too late. You know, I can't stand
the sight of you, Santouche.

SANTOUCHE: Isle of Mercy!

ISLE OF MERCY: That's not my name.

SANTOUCHE: You're not going anyplace.

ISLE OF MERCY: Here's your stink money.

SANTOUCHE: Where would you go anyway? Stay.

ISLE OF MERCY: And do what?

SANTOUCHE: I got a reputation to maintain.

ISLE OF MERCY: Look at you.
You don't even look right.
You been taking drugs?

SANTOUCHE: I won't let you go.

ISLE OF MERCY: Santouche, I won't stay.

SANTOUCHE: You can't let me down.

ISLE OF MERCY: I'm going. Good bye.

SANTOUCHE: I won't let you.

ISLE OF MERCY: You gonna kill me?

SANTOUCHE: I can't let it happen.

ISLE OF MERCY: Why don't you kill me, too,
Santouche? You'd better, because
that's the only way I'm going
to stay here.

SANTOUCHE: You shut up.

ISLE OF MERCY: Yeah. I'll shut up. So long, Santouche.

SANTOUCHE: You stay.

ISLE OF MERCY: What are you going to do, Santouche,
shoot me in the back? Well, go right
ahead, if you want to. I don't give a crap.

SANTOUCHE: Hold on, Isle of Mercy.

ISLE OF MERCY: So long.

(He shoots her in the back.)

SANTOUCHE: I told you. *(Pause)*
Dumb thing to do. *(Pause)*
Everybody telling me what to do.
Got my pride. People won't leave you alone. *(Pause)*
Got no respect. That's the trouble. *(Pause)*
Who the hell you think you are, fancy lady?
(Pause)
Busted my watch, you did. *(Pause)*
People get what they deserve.

(Pause)

FIRST CHILD: Going to kill everybody, mister?

SANTOUCHE: Who's that?

FIRST CHILD: Going to kill everybody, mister?

SANTOUCHE: Who're you talking to?

SECOND CHILD: You gonna kill me, mister?

SANTOUCHE: Who're you, kid? Hey!
You! Where're you hiding?

FIRST CHILD: You gonna kill both of us, mister?

SANTOUCHE: You better shut your mouth, kid...

SECOND CHILD: You gonna kill everybody, mister?

SANTOUCHE: Little son-of-a-bitch...

FIRST CHILD: You gonna kill everybody, mister?

SANTOUCHE: SHUT UP, YOU LITTLE SHITHEAD!

SECOND CHILD: You gonna kill me, mister?

SANTOUCHE: Leave me alone, or I will!

FIRST CHILD: You going to kill me, mister?

SANTOUCHE: Fuck, how many of you are there?

SECOND CHILD: You gonna kill everybody, mister?

SANTOUCHE: Stop it!

FIRST CHILD: You gonna kill everybody, mister?

SANTOUCHE: LEAVE ME ALONE!

SECOND CHILD: You gonna kill everyone, mister?

SANTOUCHE: GODDAMN, COCKSUCKING,
MOTHERFUCKING, SHIT HEADED...

FIRST CHILD: You gonna kill everybody, mister?

SANTOUCHE: Leave me alone, god damn it...

SECOND CHILD: You gonna kill everybody, mister?

SANTOUCHE: Hell.... What's the use? *(He sinks to the ground.)*

CHORUS: You gonna kill everyone, mister?
You gonna kill everyone, mister?
You gonna kill everyone, mister?

You gonna kill everyone, mister?
You gonna kill everyone, mister?

END OF PLAY

www.ingramcontent.com/pod-product-compliance
Ingram Content Group UK Ltd.
Pitfield, Milton Keynes, MK11 3LW, UK
UKHW020136250726
13967UKWH00002B/695

9 780881 453799